EMPTY NEST JOURNAL

30 Points and Prompts to Navigate the Uncharted Waters

By
Kim C. Steadman

Lifter Upper/Grand Prairie, TX

Lifter Upper
PO BOX 543211
Grand Prairie, TX 75054
To learn more about the author, visit
www.KimSteadman.com

Ordering Information:
Quantity sales. Special discounts are available on quantity purchases by corporations, associations, and others. For details, contact the "Special Sales Department" at the address above.
Empty Nest Journal / Kim Steadman -- 1st ed.
ISBN-13: 978-0-9983419-5-8

Contents

Ready, Set, Sail! 1

30 Points and Prompts 9

Day 1: What is your favorite weather season,
and why? 10

Day 2: Describe your first job. 12

Day 3: What is something you have always
wanted to do, but haven't? 14

Day 4: What is the one thing you must have? ..16

Day 5: What song do you feel was your theme
song when you were a teenager? 18

Day 6: What would you do if someone just gave
you $1 million?..20

Day 7: When you were a little girl and played
"pretend" what did you pretend to be?.............22

Day 8: You are the one who ____. 24

Day 9: What was your favorite subject in
elementary school? 26

Day 10: Who is someone you would like to know,
and why? 28

Day 11: Where would go if you could travel free
to anyplace in the world?..................................30

Day 12: What's the first historical event you remember? 32

Day 13: What is your favorite type of weather? Why? 34

Day 14: What would you like your life to be like one year from now?..36

Day 15: When you were little, what did you want to be when you grew up? 38

Day 16: If you could give your younger self some advice, what would it be? 40

Day 17: What cartoon did you like most as a child? Why? 42

Day 18: The best book I ever read was ___.......44

Day 19: What has been one of your greatest life accomplishments?...46

Day 20: Describe your perfect regular day. 48

Day 21: Do you have a financial goal? What is it? 50

Day 22: Which school teacher made the most impression on you? Why? 52

Day 23: Describe your perfect vacation day in detail. 54

Day 24: If you could go back in time anywhere and anytime where/when would you go and why? 56

Day 25: What type of environment do you feel most peaceful? 58

Day 26: How do you see your life five years from now? The same or different?...........................60

Day 27: What's your favorite quote? Why? 62

Day 28: What are your top 5 personal goals? ..64

Day 29: What is your hobby? Why do you enjoy it?..66

Day 30: What can you do in your current situation to be more joyful?...............................68

Setting the Course 70

I dedicate this book to

My husband, Stan whose unwavering faith in me has always been the wind beneath my wings.

My son, Matthew - you will always be my 'baby.'

Chapter 1

Ready, Set, Sail!

READY

Do you write in journals? Or is this notion intriguing because it's centered around a topic you are struggling with - the empty nest life transition?

I encourage you to remove any preconceived notions in case you think journals are some "airy-fairy" idea. A statistic I read sealed the deal for me about using journals during the empty nest transition. On a forum for Empty Nesters, 98% of the members found that writing was one thing that helped them through this phase of life. That's a pretty strong success rate to me!

My journal days began with diaries. The cute little pink ones with a golden lock on the right-hand side. I didn't have brothers or sisters who would have tried to take a glimpse at my heart-thoughts. I still locked the pages and hid my key.

When I was a pre-teen, the inspiring and historical book "The Diary of Anne Frank" spoke to my heart. She stated, "I want a dear friend, that I can share my innermost thoughts with." We moved out to a country house on a deserted, dead end road. It was a far, far away place from the suburb life I had known. Fields, woods, and wildlife soon surrounded me. They all became my friends after school and on the weekends.

While some teenage girls would have thrown a hissy-fit, I loved the new environment. I wasn't in the "in" crowd, being more of an introvert. This move allowed me to be more to myself, collect my thoughts, read and explore the countryside. I also discovered the world of journals and creative writing. The written word became my true, dear friend.

Through the years I continued the journey of writing in journals. I found later in my life that there was no dearer a friend than the friend of "self."   I shared my innermost thoughts to myself and expressed them on paper. It has continued always to be soul searching and a growth experience for me.

One of my journal discoveries, while our son was in high school, was for me, a new type of journal. It was called "morning page journals" which I read about in the book   "The Artist's Way Starter Kit" by Julia Cameron. I was a little hesitant about those "morning pages" at first due to giving up sleep in my already hectic schedule.   But, I started writing them, and I soon found out that I loved getting up in the morning to write!

Our son left for college and I lived the Empty Nest phase.   I leaned heavily on my journal writing.   I reconnected with thoughts and ideas after years of putting some them on the back burner as "Mom."   As I opened my heart and eyes, I used my written words to guide me through the uncharted waters of the empty nest years.

SET

You may have discussed or researched about this new phase of life. You most likely discovered, as I did, that every mom reacts to the empty nest transition in your unique way. There is no right or wrong way to respond because it is such a different phase of life for each woman.   In fact, sometimes it's hard for moms to open up and express their feelings to the folks closest to them. You know, it's that whole super-woman-I-can-take-on-the-world mentality that we sometimes have.

You may find yourself anonymously reaching out on forums for guidance and help. If that's a way that helps you, then, by all means, explore their advice. My only suggestion and prayer for you is this one thing. If you start to feel as though you can't cope with life during this phase of life, please reach out to a medical professional. I'm not one and am not going to pretend that I have all the answers (yes, Mom's usually do, but not this time.)

The bottom line is that every mom wants the same thing at the end of the Empty Nest Journey:

· To be happy, not sad.
· To know your life has a purpose.

Hopefully, you have decided that you are ready to embrace the change that is ahead of you. You've decided that you don't want to be one of those mom's crying every time you walk by your son or daughter's room. You don't want to mope around the house. You want to live this new phase. You just don't know where to start.

But, you may be on the other side of the coin and ecstatic and happy for your kid's new journey. You are very excited to have all this free time to yourself – but you are at a loss to the answer of "what's next?"

And, you may have a deep down feeling in your gut. A nagging sense of "I know there is more to life" and you are searching and praying for some guidance and answers.

It is here is where I hope you find help. Nestled in the pages of this journal as you answer prompts and respond to topics.

SAIL

Here's how to use this journal. If you have never written journals or diaries before, this will be a new experience. Remember, you are never too old to learn something new.

Several scriptures in the Bible that tell us to forget our past. Those are the wisdom scriptures. We need them when we reflect on our mistakes and need to let go and become the new creature in Jesus Christ.

But, when we are a mom who's poured our entire lives into our children our past can sometimes unlock our future. Yes, our yesteryears, along with our present shapes our future.

This journal contains past, present and future prompts awaiting your daily answer. Coupled with a space to write a personal prayer for the day. There's also room to draw and doodle. You will find yourself exploring into areas of your life you haven't thought about in a long time.

By the end of the 30 days, my prayer is that the prompts spark an idea. Something you want to try, a place you want to go, a project you want to start..

Your waters may be uncharted, but I have faith dear one that you will navigate them well.

Chapter 2

30 Points and Prompts

Day 1: What is your favorite weather season, and why?

Date:_____

 My prayer today...

Day 2: Describe your first job.

Date:_____

My prayer today...

13

Day 3: What is something you have always wanted to do, but haven't?

Date:_____

My prayer today...

Day 4: What is the one thing you must have?

Date:_____

My prayer today...

Day 5: What song do you feel was your theme song when you were a teenager?

Date:_____

18

 My prayer today...

Day 6: What would you do if someone just gave you $1 million?

Date:_____

My prayer today...

Day 7: When you were a little girl and played "pretend" what did you pretend to be?

Date:_____

My prayer today...

Day 8: You are the one who ___.

Date:_____

 My prayer today...

Day 9: What was your favorite subject in elementary school?

Date:_____

 My prayer today...

Day 10: Who is someone you would like to know, and why?

Date:_____

 My prayer today...

29

Day 11: Where would go if you could travel free to anyplace in the world?

Date:_____

My prayer today...

Day 12: What's the first historical event you remember?

Date:_____

 My prayer today...

33

Day 13: What is your favorite type of weather? Why?

Date:_____

 My prayer today...

Day 14: What would you like your life to be like one year from now?

Date:_____

 My prayer today...

Day 15: When you were little, what did you want to be when you grew up?

Date:_____

 My prayer today...

Day 16: If you could give your younger self some advice, what would it be?

Date:_____

My prayer today...

Day 17: What cartoon did you like most as a child? Why?

Date:_____

My prayer today...

Day 18: The best book I ever read was __.

Date:_____

My prayer today...

Day 19: What has been one of your greatest life accomplishments?

Date:_____

My prayer today...

Day 20: Describe your perfect regular day.

Date:_____

 My prayer today...

Day 21: Do you have a financial goal? What is it?

Date:_____

My prayer today...

Day 22: Which school teacher made the most impression on you? Why?

Date:_____

My prayer today...

Day 23: Describe your perfect vacation day in detail.

Date:_____

 My prayer today...

Day 24: If you could go back in time anywhere and anytime where/when would you go and why?

Date:_____

 My prayer today...

Day 25: What type of environment do you feel most peaceful?

Date:_____

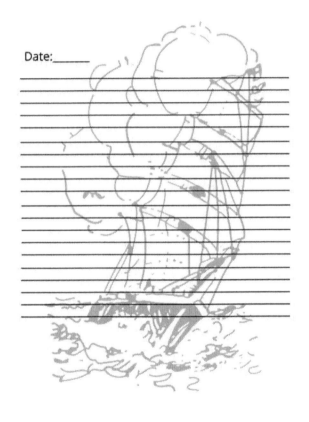

My prayer today...

Day 26: How do you see your life five years
from now? The same or different?

Date:_____

My prayer today...

Day 27: What's your favorite quote? Why?

Date:_____

My prayer today...

Day 28: What are your top 5 personal goals?

Date:_____

My prayer today...

Day 29: What is your hobby? Why do you enjoy it?

Date:_____

My prayer today...

Day 30: What can you do in your current situation to be more joyful?

Date:_____

My prayer today...

Chapter 3

Setting the Course

You've come to the end of your 30-day journal, and I hope you had some 'aha' moments of revelation.

The whole idea of the Empty Nest Journal is three-fold. The journal prompts were specifically chosen to help you:

- Reflect on the Past
- Evaluate the Present
- Plan for the Future

As you go back and read what you wrote, look for something that jumps out at you. Was there a prompt that caused you to think of an old hobby you used to enjoy? Or perhaps you thought about something new you have always wanted to try.

Use the responses in your journal as a tool to help you navigate through the empty nest. Look at what you wrote and find new ideas and a renewed, fresh purpose. Decide in your heart "Yes, this is a new phase in life. But it's a transition, and I've successfully navigated other transitions before."

I encourage you to continue the practice and write in your journal while you transition. Pray before you write in your journal. Ask God to reveal himself to you and give you insight.

ABOUT THE AUTHOR

Kim Steadman is a cubicle-nation escapee. After ending her corporate life, she went home to pursue childhood dreams. She encourages women to redesign their lives when the nest empties. With the inspiration of the Texas sun, she writes to the heart and soul of women and as a legacy to her grandson.

Readers received her book, The Creative Prayer Journal, with glowing reviews. She is also the author of the "Denver, The Recycled Dog" series. You can read about her newest writing projects at www.KimSteadman.com

49199117R00050

Made in the USA
Middletown, DE
09 October 2017